RAIN FORESTS

ENDANGERED
BIOMES

DONNA LATHAM

Nomad Press
A division of Nomad Communications
10 9 8 7 6 5 4 3 2 1

Printed by Regal Printing Limited in China,
June 2011, Job Number 1105033
ISBN: 978-1-936313-49-5

Educational Consultant, Marla Conn

Questions regarding the ordering of this book should be addressed to
Independent Publishers Group
814 N. Franklin St.
Chicago, IL 60610
www.ipgbook.com

Nomad Press
2456 Christian St.
White River Junction, VT 05001
www.nomadpress.net

Image Credits

Corbisimages.com/ Catherine Karnow, cover; Paul Souders, 3.

©iStockphoto.com/ Mark Kostich, title page, 25; Jussi Santaniemi, 1; Jay Rysavy, 1; ziggymaj, 5; 2 designs, 6, 13, 14; Elena Kalistratova, 6; Alexander Chaikin, 6; Karel Broz, 7; Morley Read 7, 8, 13; Mike Bentley, 7; arlindo71, 8; Matthew Cole, 8; Vassiliy Vishnevskiy, 8; Rob Broek, 9; Jessie DiBlasi, 10; Michał Saganowski, 11; Jim Jurica, 11; Joakim Leroy, 11, 12, 26; ZoneCreative, 12; Eric Isselée, 13, 18; Mark Kostich, 14; Judy Worley, 15; George Clerk, 15; grafxcom, 15; Khuong Hoang, 16; Joakim Leroy, 16; 1 design, 16; Ameng Wu, 16; muharrem öner, 17; leonard_c, 18; Yong Hian Lim, 18; only_fabrizio, 19; Robyn Mackenzie, 20; enviromantic, 20; mypokcik, 20; Aleksandar Kolundzija, 21; BlueOrange Studio, 22; Kadir Barcin, 23; Richard Lathulerie, 23; Keiichi Hiki, 24; Lucía Cóppola, 26.

CONTENTS

What Is a Biome?

Grab your backpack! You're about to embark on an exciting expedition to explore one of Earth's major **biomes**: the **tropical rainforest**!

A biome is a large natural area with a distinctive **climate** and **geology**. The desert is a biome. The ocean and tundra are biomes. So is the tropical rainforest. Biomes are the earth's communities.

Did You Know?

Scientists don't agree on how many biomes there are. Some divide the earth into five biomes. Others argue for 12.

biome: a large natural area with a distinctive climate, geology, and set of water resources. A biome's plants and animals are adapted for life there.

tropical rainforest: a dense forest of tall trees near the equator.

climate: average weather patterns in an area over many years.

geology: the rocks, minerals, and physical structure of an area.

adapt: changes a plant or animal makes to survive in new or different conditions.

ecosystem: a community of living and nonliving things and their environment. Living things are plants, animals, and insects. Nonliving things are soil, rocks, and water.

environment: everything in nature, living and nonliving.

Each biome has its own biodiversity, which is the range of living things **adapted** for life there. It also contains many **ecosystems**. In an ecosystem, living and nonliving things interact with their **environment**.

Teamwork keeps the system balanced and working. Earth's biomes are connected together, creating a vast web of life.

2

Landscape and Climate

You'll need an umbrella in the world's rainiest biome. Tropical rainforests receive 50 to 260 inches of rain each year (125 to 660 centimeters). Rain falls almost every day. But leave your coat at home!

The climate in the tropical rainforest is about the same year round. It never snows or gets cold. There may be a short season with less rain, but that is the only change from season to season.

of the Tropical Rainforests

It's hot and humid in the rainforest. The average temperature during the day is 86 to 95 degrees Fahrenheit (30 to 35 degrees Celsius).

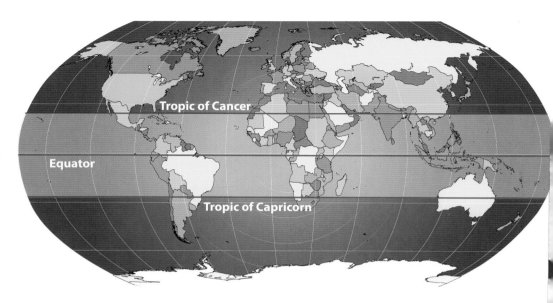

Tropical rainforests are located near the equator, between the Tropic of Cancer and the Tropic of Capricorn. You'll find tropical rainforests in Australia, Central and South America, the Pacific Islands, Southeast Asia, and West Africa.

Did You Know?

The equator is an imaginary line around the widest surface of the earth, at its center. The Tropic of Cancer and the Tropic of Capricorn are two lines of **latitude**, above and below the equator.

There are four levels of every tropical rainforest: the **emergent layer**, **canopy**, **understory**, and **forest floor**. Different plants and animals live at each layer.

Although rainforests cover only 6 percent of the earth's landmass, half of the planet's animal and plant **species** make their homes there.

Squirrel monkey

Gecko

Words to Know

latitude: imaginary lines around the earth parallel to the equator.

emergent layer: the tallest layer in the rainforest.

canopy: an umbrella of trees over the forest.

understory: the layer that grows under the forest canopy.

forest floor: the ground under the trees in the forest.

species: a type of animal or plant.

6

here: The soil in tropical rainforests is low in **nutrients**. Pounding rains flush them away.

there: The soil in deciduous forests is rich in nutrients. Deciduous forests are found mostly north of the tropics. These trees shed their leaves each year.

Nutrients in the rainforest are found in the living plants and in the leaf litter on the forest floor. When dead plants and animals fall to the ground, they **decompose**.

Their nutrients are recycled by **decomposers**, ready for living plants to take out of the soil and use again. In this hot, moist environment, decomposition is speedy.

Insects are the largest group of animals in the rainforest.

Words to Know

nutrients: substances that living things need to live and grow.

decompose: to break down or rot.

decomposers: bacteria, fungi, worms, and insects that break down dead plants and animals.

Plants Growing in the

The top level is the emergent layer, where treetops burst out of the rainforest. Colossal **broadleaf** trees tower 250 feet high (76 meters).

These green giants support their own weight as well as the load of all the critters that live in them. How do these trees hold themselves up in shallow, soggy soil? They grow thick roots called **buttresses** that fan out as natural supports.

Buttresses

The emergent layer gets pummeled with fierce winds and heavy rains. It endures incredible heat.

Beneath the emergent layer is the cooler, damp canopy. It is shaped like an open umbrella. Here, broadleaf trees stretch toward the sun, some peaking at 90 feet (27 meters).

Rainforest Have Adapted

Words to Know

broadleaf: having wide, flat leaves.

buttresses: thick roots above the ground that support tall trees.

Orchids

The understory is the forest beneath the canopy. Smaller trees and shrubs compete for space here, where sunlight is limited. Plants grow gigantic leaves. This adaptation allows them to capture as much of the sun's energy as possible.

Patchy lichens, ferns, and delicate orchids grow in this level too.

Did You Know?

Lianas are woody vines that dangle throughout the canopy and understory. As the vines grow, they weave themselves around trees like bungee cords and climb high to soak in the sun's rays. Lianas are so tough that people in the rainforest use them to build bridges.

Lianas

Did You Know?

Brazil nuts, coconuts, bananas, mango, papaya, and star fruit are some of the yummy foods from the rainforest.

The forest floor sprawls at the bottom. Little sunlight reaches the floor. Healthy plants need to shed water rapidly so they won't decay. Leaves are adapted with pointy tips that let rainwater drip off quickly.

You can grow tropical rainforest plants. Exotic houseplants such as African violets, Christmas cactus, prayer plants, and zebra plants are adapted to the dim light of the forest floor. They can grow in low light in homes.

Animals Living in the

The emergent layer is home to bats, butterflies, harpy eagles, howler monkeys, and snakes. What's the benefit of living way up high? It's where the most sunlight is.

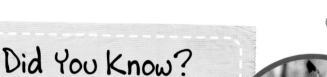

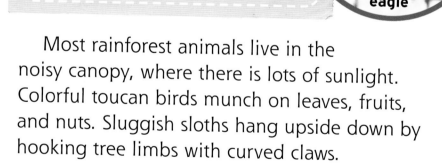

Harpy eagle

Most rainforest animals live in the noisy canopy, where there is lots of sunlight. Colorful toucan birds munch on leaves, fruits, and nuts. Sluggish sloths hang upside down by hooking tree limbs with curved claws.

Hummingbirds slip their needle-nose bills into flowers to sip sweet nectar. Many have **migrated** from colder climates for the winter.

Toucan

Rainforest Have Adapted

Words to Know

prey: an animal hunted by a predator for food.

predator: an animal that hunts another animal for food.

migrate: to move from one environment to another.

camouflage: colors or patterns that allow a plant or animal to blend in with its environment.

The red-eyed tree frog is one of the Amazon rainforest's most recognizable creatures. Suction cups on its tiny feet are adapted to cling to leaves in the canopy.

The frog's peepers provide **camouflage** called startle coloration. By shutting its green eyelids, the frog blends in with multi-colored leaves. When a snake slithers by or a bird dives down, the frog quickly opens its big red eyes. The confused predator stops long enough for the frog to make a speedy getaway into the leafy understory.

Red-eyed tree frog

14

Flying, gliding, leaping, and swinging are the best ways to travel through the canopy. Snag a sturdy liana, and swoop down to the understory. Spiders and insects offer tasty snacks for birds, lizards, snakes, and monkeys. These insects include walking sticks, beetles, bees, and army ants.

Orangutans

Central Africa's okapi is nicknamed the "forest giraffe." Its long, **prehensile** tongue is adapted for grasping and yanking leaves. And its tongue is a clue that it's related to the giraffe.

Okapi

Why doesn't the okapi have a giraffe's long neck and stilt–like legs?

The okapi has to dodge dangling lianas and chunky buttresses to **forage** for food. Lanky limbs and a stretchy neck would get in the way.

Giraffe

15

Words to Know

prehensile: able to grasp things.

forage: to search for food.

herbivore: an animal that eats only plants.

carnivore: an animal that eats only other animals.

anaconda: the largest living snake.

food chain: a community of plants and animals where each is eaten by another higher up in the chain.

What Eats What?

Seeds and fruits tumble to the forest floor from the canopy and understory. **Herbivores** devour them before they decay in the tropical heat. **Carnivores**, including jaguars and **anacondas**, prowl in this dark level. Plants and animals are all part of the **food chain**.

Jaguar

16

Environmental Threats

Deforestation is the largest threat to this biome. People clear land for mining, farming, and to build homes and dams. Because the soil is so poor, the rainforest cannot grow back once it's cleared.

Climate change is one effect of deforestation. The entire world's climate depends on the rainforest. Scientists have nicknamed tropical rainforests "the lungs of the planet." Through **photosynthesis**, plants clean carbon dioxide from the air. Plants then release oxygen, which people and animals need to breathe and live.

The rainforests provide 20 percent of the world's oxygen. But because of deforestation, Earth's lungs are shrinking—fast.

Greenhouse gases such as carbon dioxide, methane, and water vapor help form our **atmosphere**. They permit the sun's rays to enter, and then they trap the heat. More greenhouse gases trap more heat.

Words to Know

deforestation: when whole forests are chopped down.

climate change: a change in the world's weather and climate.

photosynthesis: the process through which plants create food, using light as a source of energy.

greenhouse gas: a gas that traps heat in the earth's atmosphere.

atmosphere: the mixture of gases around our planet.

Chameleon

18

Biodiversity at Risk

Habitat destruction for thousands of species is another serious effect of deforestation. Many species live nowhere else on the planet. Some scientists believe that about 35 rainforest species become **extinct** each day.

Words to Know

habitat: a plant or animal's home.

extinct: the death of an entire species so that it no longer exists.

erosion: when land is worn away by wind or water.

One quarter of our medicines come from rainforest plants. Quinine comes from the bark of the Cinchona tree, and is used to treat malaria. The rosy periwinkle provides the main ingredient in an important cancer-fighting drug. Who knows what medicines might be waiting to be discovered in the plants and animals of the rainforest?

Many plant and animal species depend on the Amazon River flooding each year during the rainy season. But the flooding is threatened by deforestation, **erosion**, and dams that change the flow of water.

Path to Extinction

Rare: Only a small number of the species is alive. Scientists are concerned about the future of the species.

Threatened: The species lives, but its numbers will likely continue to decline. It will probably become endangered.

Endangered: The species is in danger of extinction in the very near future.

Extinct in the Wild: Some members of the species live, but only in protected captivity and not out in the wild.

Extinct: The species has completely died out. It has disappeared from the planet.

Tarsier

The Future of the

People are increasingly aware of the delicate balance of life on Earth. Many are devoted to conserving our natural resources and preserving our biomes. But little by little, every day, we lose more of the world's rainforest.

Tropical trees, including mahogany and ebony, are valued for their wood. But even selective logging damages the rainforest. Its roads open the land up to farmers and large companies.

The power of rivers is used to generate electricity. But building massive dams destroys huge areas of the rainforest.

Words to Know

selective: choosing some, but not all, of something.

sustainable: a way of using a resource that does not damage or destroy it.

Rainforest

When people see the rainforest having more value to them than just its wood, they will preserve it.

Changing the flow of rivers hurts ecosystems far beyond the dam.

Fair trade is a business model that pays farmers a fair price for their products, such as coffee and chocolate. It helps them farm in a way that is **sustainable**.

Conservation Challenge

Think about what You can do to benefit the environment. What actions can you take? How can you inspire others to do the same?

The way your family spends its money can make a difference to the future of the rainforest. Look for products with the fair trade label.

When you encourage your parents to choose only sustainable products from the rainforest, you are helping to save the rainforest.

25

- Buying fair trade coffee, chocolate, and nuts helps to build the market for these products. It supports the local people of the rainforest biome. If people can support themselves with sustainable products then they won't have to cut the forest for its wood.

Bougainvillea

- Spread the word about buying products made from sustainable wood. Don't buy anything made with tropical wood.

- Don't buy anything made from endangered species. Avoid items made with ivory, feathers, crocodile skins, or turtle shells.

Sustainable use of the rainforest is the only way to save it. We can benefit from the trees without destroying them.

Glossary

adapt: changes a plant or animal makes to survive in new or different conditions.

anaconda: the largest living snake.

atmosphere: the mixture of gases around our planet.

biodiversity: the range of living things in an ecosystem.

biome: a large natural area with a distinctive climate, geology, and set of water resources. A biome's plants and animals are adapted for life there.

broadleaf: having wide, flat leaves.

buttresses: thick roots above the ground that support tall trees.

camouflage: colors or patterns that allow a plant or animal to blend in with its environment.

canopy: an umbrella of trees over the forest.

carnivore: an animal that eats only other animals.

climate: average weather patterns in an area over many years.

climate change: a change in the world's weather and climate.

decompose: to break down or rot.

decomposers: bacteria, fungi, worms, and insects that break down dead plants and animals.

deforestation: when whole forests are chopped down.

ecosystem: a community of living and nonliving things and their environment. Living things are plants, animals, and insects. Nonliving things are soil, rocks, and water.

emergent layer: the tallest layer in the rainforest.

environment: everything in nature, living and nonliving.

erosion: when land is worn away by wind or water.

extinct: the death of an entire species so that it no longer exists.

food chain: a community of plants and animals where each is eaten by another higher up in the chain.

forage: to search for food.

forest floor: the ground under the trees in the forest.

geology: the rocks, minerals, and physical structure of an area.

greenhouse gas: a gas that traps heat in the earth's atmosphere.

habitat: a plant or animal's home.

herbivore: an animal that eats only plants.

latitude: imaginary lines around the earth parallel to the equator.

migrate: to move from one environment to another.

nutrients: substances that living things need to live and grow.

photosynthesis: the process through which plants create food, using light as a source of energy.

predator: an animal that hunts another animal for food.

prehensile: able to grasp things.

prey: an animal hunted by a predator for food.

selective: choosing some, but not all, of something.

species: a type of animal or plant.

sustainable: a way of using a resource that does not damage or destroy it.

tropical rainforest: a dense forest of tall trees near the equator.

Tropic of Cancer: a line of latitude north of the equator.

Tropic of Capricorn: a line of latitude south of the equator.

understory: the layer that grows under the forest canopy.

Further Investigations

Cherry, Lynn. *How We Know What We Know About Our Changing Climate: Scientists and Kids Explore Global Warming*. Dawn Publications, 2008.

Latham, Donna. *Amazing Biome Projects You Can Build Yourself*. Nomad Press, 2009.

Reilly, Kathleen M. *Planet Earth: 25 Environmental Projects You Can Build Yourself*. Nomad Press, 2008.

Rothschild, David. *Earth Matters: An Encyclopedia of Ecology*. DK Publishing, 2008.

Smithsonian Institution National Museum of Natural History
www.mnh.si.edu
Washington, D.C.

US National Parks www.us-parks.com

Enchanted Learning, Biomes
www.enchantedlearning.com/biomes

Energy Efficiency and Renewable Energy
www.eere.energy.gov/kids

Geography for Kids www.kidsgeo.com

Inch in a Pinch: Saving the Earth
www.inchinapinch.com

Kids Do Ecology
www.kids.nceas.ucsb.edu

Library ThinkQuest
www.thinkquest.org

National Geographic Kids
www.kids.nationalgeographic.com

NOAA for Kids
www.oceanservice.noaa.gov/kids

Oceans for Youth
www.oceansforyouth.org

The Nature Conservancy
www.nature.org

World Wildlife Federation
www.panda.org

Index